Elf~help for Coping with Cancer

D0826722

Elf-help for Coping with Cancer

written by
Joel Schorn

illustrated by
R.W. Alley

ONE
CARING
PLACE
Abbey Press

Text © 2007 by Joel Schorn
Illustrations © 2007 by Saint Meinrad Archabbey
Published by One Caring Place
Abbey Press
St. Meinrad, Indiana 47577

Library of Congress Catalog Number
2007922540

ISBN 978-0-87029-405-1

Printed in the United States of America

Foreword

A diagnosis of cancer touches every part of your life. Like a stone thrown into a pond, cancer ripples through your life and the lives of those around you. You have new fears and new feelings. You face a long and uncertain road. You wonder what life and even God has in store for you. Through your treatment, you'll experience some pain and a good deal of anxiety.

Elf-help for Coping with Cancer offers ways to meet the physical and emotional challenges of cancer. In helping you cope in a positive way with your fears, feelings, and doubts, it suggests how you can react to your illness and also act in ways that will help you heal. It will also help you see how having cancer, despite the limitations and downright terrors it may present, can offer opportunities to grow closer to God and those around you, and to focus on what's really important.

May this little book help you face cancer with acceptance, hope, and love.

1.

Finding out you have cancer can be devastating. In time, you will get past the shock and be able to focus on getting better and living with your new situation.

2.

You have fears about the future, how you'll feel, what will happen to your family. It's good to identify and acknowledge your fears, and even talk about them. Getting them out in the open makes them seem less frightening.

3.

You have a long battle ahead of you, but whatever happens, don't give up! God is walking with you.

4.

Real courage isn't being unafraid. It's not allowing your fears to conquer you. It's OK to be afraid as you confront this disease. You'll find the courage to do what you need to do.

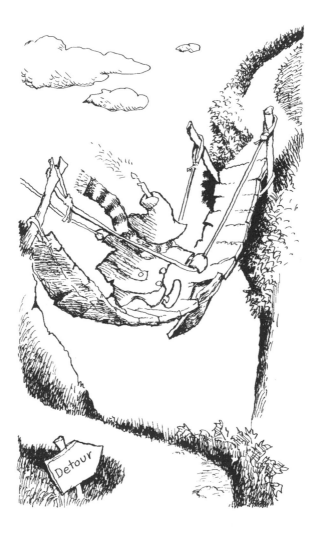

5.

It's normal to experience "negative" emotions when you have cancer: fear, grief, and anger—at the disease, at doctors, at life, even at God. Let yourself have these "negative" feelings. Find "positive" ways to express them.

6.

You'll go through periods of telling yourself this can't be happening or it's not as bad as it seems. Like fear, anger, and sadness, it's OK to just want the cancer to go away. Turn that desire into hope and strength.

7.

Cancer can lead to feelings of hopelessness, as if life no longer has purpose. But your life is still full. Your loved ones, your faith in God, even coping with your illness, give you plenty of ways to find meaning in your life.

8.

The stress and anxiety of having cancer might make you depressed. It's not wrong for you to react this way. If depression becomes overwhelming, ask for help from counselors and your health-care team.

9.

Whatever you're feeling, there's no "correct" way to react to cancer. Everyone is different, and your way of coping will be your own.

10.

It's perfectly natural to ask yourself, "Why did this have to happen to me?" But cancer can happen to anyone. You didn't "deserve" it. It happened, and the best thing is to focus on getting better.

11.

Be prepared to give yourself
time and do lots of waiting.
God and others will walk
with you.

12.

One day, you'll feel hopeful and confident, and the next, sad or depressed. You're going to have many ups and downs. Tell yourself that's all part of dealing with cancer.

13.

Coping with cancer is a struggle. But you will have joy, too. Celebrate your victories: a positive check-up, finishing a treatment, or just a day of feeling good.

14.

Cancer brings many changes: not only to your health, but also how you feel, how you look, your expectations, your relationships. Life will not be the same. But change presents opportunities to grow.

15.

Some of these changes will mean losses—of health, independence, lifestyle, and more. It's important to let yourself grieve your losses.

16.

You don't feel well, you can't get around as easily as you used to, you need help. Part of accepting your new life as a person with cancer is accepting your new limitations as part of who you are now.

17.

Sometimes people feel guilty or ashamed when they get cancer. If you feel this way, try some self-forgiveness. Accepting yourself is a first step toward accepting you are ill and want to get better.

18.

While your life will change,
in some ways forever, it helps
to try to live as "normal" a life
as possible. Keep up with your
routines as much as you can.
Do things you've always
enjoyed.

19.

Though it sounds strange, many people with cancer see it as a gift. Be grateful for what illness teaches you, and for the ways in which you are healthy.

20.

Cancer treatment is better than ever. Have hope that you can survive and live a full life.

21.

Find out as much you can about your specific form of cancer. The more you know, the less helpless and afraid you'll feel. You'll be able to make better decisions, too.

22.

Work with members of
your health-care team.
Communication will assist
them with your treatment,
and you in dealing with
your illness.

23.

Decisions about your care are ultimately yours. Talk with your doctors and your family, and then make the decisions you feel are right in your heart and mind.

24.

You are not alone. People are there to help you—medical professionals, friends and family, health-care chaplains, counselors, your faith community, other people who have cancer. Ask for help. And always remember that God is with you.

25.

Being sick will have an effect
on those around you. Your
loved ones are afraid for you,
but they also want to help.
Have patience with them,
but also welcome their support.

26.

You can't avoid some pain and discomfort. But your health-care team will try to minimize your pain. Ask God to be with you in your pain. God hears the cries of those in distress.

27.

You might be asking yourself, "Why did God let this happen?" God is not punishing you. Believe that "all things work for good" for those who place their faith in God, even amid difficult or painful circumstances.

28.

You might also ask yourself, "Where is God?" God has not abandoned you. Have faith that God will be with you and see you through whatever happens.

29.

Ask God to heal you in body and spirit. You may not be cured as you wish, but your prayers can bring you acceptance and peace.

30.

Facing cancer or any threat to your health and life changes your priorities. Refocus on the people and things that are truly important in your life.

31.

Someone once said attitude is a little thing that makes a big difference. Having a positive attitude will go a long way toward helping you heal.

32.

What have you always
wanted to do? Use this
time to try new things.

33.

It's hard to know the future, so live your life one day at a time. Make the most of every day!

34.

Make sure you're good to yourself. Do things that are healthy. Relax and try to reduce stress. Conserve your energy.

35.

So much is going on inside you. Spend some quiet time just breathing and being in the loving presence of God.

36.

Having a serious illness can make you more aware of others who are suffering. It can make you an expert companion, guide, and listener. Show your compassion and care for others who are sick or in need.

37.

While there's nothing funny about cancer, don't forget to laugh sometimes. Laughter is good medicine.

38.

God loves you no matter what.
Welcome the love others have
for you. Give love to everyone
you meet. Love will see you
through.

Joel Schorn is a writer and editor living in Chicago. He is the author of several CareNotes and PrayerNotes published by Abbey Press.

Illustrator for the Abbey Press Elf-help Books, **R.W. Alley** also illustrates and writes children's books. He lives in Barrington, Rhode Island, with his wife, daughter, and son. See a wide variety of his works at: www.rwalley.com.

The Story of the Abbey Press Elves

The engaging figures that populate the Abbey Press "elf-help" line of publications and products first appeared in 1987 on the pages of a small self-help book called *Be-good-to-yourself Therapy*. Shaped by the publishing staff's vision and defined in R.W. Alley's inventive illustrations, they lived out the author's gentle, self-nurturing advice with charm, poignancy, and humor.

Reader response was so enthusiastic that more Elf-help Books were soon under way, a still-growing series that has inspired a line of related gift products.

The especially endearing character featured in the early books—sporting a cap with a mood-changing candle in its peak—has since been joined by a spirited female elf with flowers in her hair.

These two exuberant, sensitive, resourceful, kindhearted, lovable sprites, along with their lively elfin community, reveal what's truly important as they offer messages of joy and wonder, playfulness and co-creation, wholeness and serenity, the miracle of life and the mystery of God's love.

With wisdom and whimsy, these little creatures with long noses demonstrate the elf-help way to a rich and fulfilling life.

Elf-help Books

...adding "a little character" and a lot
of help to self-help reading!

Forgiveness Therapy	#20184
Keep-life-simple Therapy	#20185
Acceptance Therapy	#20190
Keeping-up-your-spirits Therapy	#20195
Slow-down Therapy	#20203
One-day-at-a-time Therapy	#20204
Prayer Therapy	#20206
Be-good-to-your-marriage Therapy	#20205
Be-good-to-yourself Therapy	#20255

Book price is $4.95 unless otherwise noted.
Available at your favorite gift shop or bookstore—
or directly from One Caring Place, Abbey Press
Publications, St. Meinrad, IN 47577.
Or call 1-800-325-2511.
www.carenotes.com